How Was Your Lemonade?

Seed
Learning

sweet

sour

spicy

salty

bitter

crunchy

gross

delicious

How was your
lemonade?

It was sour.

How was your soup?

It was spicy.

How was your sandwich?

It was delicious!

Let's learn about Singapore.

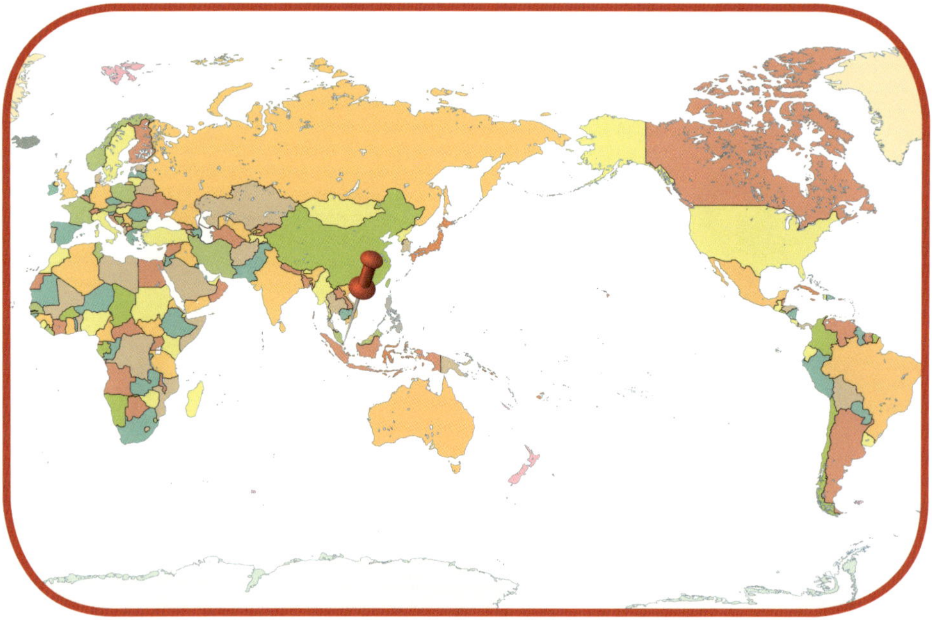

Flag of Singapore

Gardens by the Bay